ELEMENTS OF *Writing*

REVISED EDITION

Practicing the
WRITING PROCESS

WORKSHEETS
WITH ANSWER KEYS

▶ Fifth Course

D0897370

HOLT, RINEHART AND WINSTON

Harcourt Brace & Company

Austin • *New York • Orlando • Atlanta • San Francisco • Boston • Dallas • Toronto • London*

Staff Credits

Associate Director: Mescal Evler

Managing Editor: Steve Welch

Project Editors: Susan Sims Britt, Susan Lynch

Editorial Staff: *Editors,* Jonathan David Carson, Adrienne Greer; *Copy Editors,* Joseph S. Schofield IV, Atietie O. Tonwe; *Coordinators,* Susan G. Alexander, Amanda F. Beard, Rebecca Bennett, Wendy Langabeer, Marie Hoffman Price; *Support,* Ruth A. Hooker, Kelly Keeley, Margaret Sanchez, Pat Stover

Design: Christine Schueler

Editorial Permissions: Janet Harrington

Production Coordinator: Rose Degollado

Electronic Publishing Supervisor: Barbara Hudgens

Electronic Publishing Staff: Heather Jernt, *Project Coordinator*
JoAnn Brown, David Hernandez, Rina May Ouellette, Charlie Taliaferro, Ethan Thompson

Contributing Writers

Judith Austin-Mills
Bill Martin
Matthew H. Pangborn
Raymond Teague

Copyright © by Holt, Rinehart and Winston, Inc.

All rights reserved. No part of this publication may be reproduced or transmitted in any form or by any means, electronic or mechanical, including photocopy, recording, or any information storage and retrieval system, without permission in writing from the publisher.

Permission is hereby granted to reproduce Blackline Masters in this publication in complete pages for instructional use and not for resale by any teacher using ELEMENTS OF WRITING.

Printed in the United States of America

ISBN 0-03-051192-5

1 2 3 4 5 085 00 99 98 97

Contents

HRW material copyrighted under notice appearing earlier in this work.

To the Teacher

The teacher support provided by the *Annotated Teacher's Edition* is further reinforced by the *Teaching Resources.*

The *Teaching Resources* have been designed to help you in your classroom—where the demands on your time and energy are great—to deal with each student as an individual.

This booklet, *Practicing the Writing Process,* contains copying masters developed to provide practice in and reinforcement of the concepts and skills presented in the Writing Handbook, Chapters 1–3, of the *Pupil's Edition.* Worksheets are organized by chapter, and answer keys are provided at the end of each chapter.

Practicing the Writing Process is the first in a series of eight booklets comprising the *Teaching Resources.*

- ***Practicing the Writing Process***
- *Strategies for Writing*
- *Word Choice and Sentence Style*
- *Language Skills Practice and Assessment*
- *Academic and Workplace Skills*
- *Holistic Scoring: Prompts and Models*
- *Portfolio Assessment*
- *Practice for Assessment in Reading, Vocabulary, and Spelling*

HRW material copyrighted under notice appearing earlier in this work.

Chapter 1: Writing and Thinking

Freewriting and Brainstorming

When you **freewrite,** you jot down whatever pops into your head. To freewrite,

1. Set a limit of three to five minutes. Keep writing until the time's up.

2. Start with a word or topic that's important to you.

3. Don't worry about complete sentences or proper punctuation. It's OK if your thoughts are disorganized or if you repeat yourself.

4. Occasionally, choose one key word or phrase from your freewriting and use it as a starting point for more writing. Such **focused freewriting,** or **looping,** will allow you to move from what you've already written to something new.

Brainstorming, a type of free association, is another way to generate ideas. To brainstorm,

1. Write a word, phrase, or topic on your paper or on the board.

2. Jot down *every* idea that comes to your mind.

3. Don't stop to evaluate; just keep going until you run out of ideas.

Exercise A   Choose one of the following general subjects. Brainstorm about this subject by yourself or with a few classmates. On the lines below, list all the writing topics that you found during your brainstorming session.

Subjects: basketball   Mexican history and culture   computers

class trips   shopping malls   space stations

Subject chosen for brainstorming: _____

Possible topics gathered from brainstorming: _____

_____

_____

_____

Exercise B   Choose another subject from the list given in Exercise A. Freewrite on this subject. Put your pen or pencil to the paper and write whatever comes into your mind about the subject. Don't worry about grammar, usage, or mechanics.

_____

_____

_____

_____

_____

_____

_____

_____

HRW material copyrighted under notice appearing earlier in this work.

Chapter 1: Writing and Thinking

Clustering and Questioning

Clustering, like brainstorming, is a free-association technique. However, unlike brainstorming, clustering shows the connections between ideas. Clustering is sometimes called *webbing* or *making connections*. To cluster,

1. Write a subject in the center of your paper. Draw a circle around it.

2. In the space around the circle, write all the words or ideas that come to mind as you think about the subject. Circle each addition, and then draw a line connecting it to the original circled subject or to another circled idea.

You can also use the **5W-How? questions** to investigate some subjects. To do so, ask *Who? What? Where? When? Why?* and *How?* about your subject.

Exercise A   Choose one of the following subjects or one of your own choice. Write the subject in the center circle below. Then create a cluster diagram by thinking of ideas related to the subject.

Subjects: school spirit   a family tradition   robotics

Fridays   situation comedies   a current news event

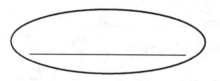

Exercise B   Choose another subject from the list given in Exercise A or come up with a subject of your own. Write that subject. Then write six questions about the subject. Begin your questions with the words *Who, What, Where, When, Why,* and *How.*
Subject:

1. Who _____ ?

2. What _____ ?

3. Where _____ ?

4. When _____ ?

5. Why _____ ?

6. How _____ ?

HRW material copyrighted under notice appearing earlier in this work.

Chapter 1: Writing and Thinking

Purpose, Audience, and Tone

Your **purpose** is your reason for writing. You can write to express feelings; to be creative; to explain, explore, or inform; or to persuade.

Your **audience** is the people who will read or listen to your writing. The audience you choose will affect what you say and how you say it. When writing for a particular audience, you need to consider what the audience already knows about your subject, what will interest that audience, and what level of language will be appropriate.

Your **tone** is your attitude toward the subject and toward your readers. The tone of a piece of writing can often be described in a single word: *lively, sarcastic, amused,* or *serious,* for example. To create a particular tone, you must be careful in your choice of words, details, sentence lengths, and sentence structures.

Exercise   Read each of the following paragraphs. Then record its purpose, a possible audience for it, and its tone.

   1. Before we even started the fourth quarter, I knew it was all over. Angie,

our leading scorer, wasn't performing. The Cougars still looked fresh and fierce,

while we looked like a bunch of amateurs. I felt so frustrated I could have cried.

Purpose: _____

Audience: _____

Tone: _____

   2. Feel the luxury. Harness the power. Own the best. The legendary Auriga is

simply the finest car you'll ever buy.

Purpose: _____

Audience: _____

Tone: _____

   3. Want to burn down 10,000 acres of forest in a jiffy? Well, it's easy to do. Just

leave a campfire burning. Just be a little careless the next time you're in the woods

on a hot, dry summer day. Anyone can do it. It's a snap.

Purpose: _____

Audience: _____

Tone: _____

HRW material copyrighted under notice appearing earlier in this work.

Reading and Listening with a Focus

Reading with a focus is one way to collect information for a piece of writing. To read with a focus,

1. Give the possible source of information a "once-over." Look for key words in the index. Check the table of contents. Look at chapter headings and subheadings.

2. Skim until you find a passage that deals with your topic. Then slow down and take notes. Make sure to record publication information so that you will be able to cite your source.

To listen with a focus,

1. Think ahead. Make an outline of information you need, or prepare questions to ask.

2. In an interview, concentrate on the question being answered. Don't let your mind wander to the next question.

3. Take notes even if you are also making a recording. Don't try to write down every word. Use phrases and abbreviations, and listen for main ideas and significant details.

Exercise A   You are writing a paper about skyscrapers. Find a book about the history of architecture. Using the book, list the following information.

1. key words in the index: _____   _____

_____   _____

_____   _____

2. chapters worth reading or skimming:

_____   _____

Exercise B   Skim one of the chapters of the book you used in Exercise A. While skimming, list headings, charts, and illustrations that will be helpful for your report.

_____

_____

_____

_____

_____

Exercise C   You are about to watch a documentary on the historic *Apollo 11* moon landing in 1969. Prepare yourself for listening by making a list of three ideas to listen for or three questions that you want answered.

1. _____

2. _____

3. _____

HRW material copyrighted under notice appearing earlier in this work.

Arranging Ideas

You can arrange your ideas by using chronological order, spatial order, order of importance, or ligical order.

When using **chronological order,** you present events as they happen in time. You use chronological order when you write narration. Stories, narrative poems, explanations of processes, history, biography, and drama all often use chronological order.

When using **spatial order,** you present objects according to their locations. For example, you might describe objects in order *from near to far, from left to right,* or *from top to bottom.*

When using **order of importance,** you present ideas or details from least to most important or vice versa. You can use order of importance when you write descriptions, explanations, persuasions, or evaluations.

When using **logical order,** you relate items and groups. You use logical order when you define, classify, compare, or contrast.

Exercise   Read the topics below and decide which of the four types of order discussed above would be most suitable for developing each topic. On the lines provided, write **C** for chronological, **S** for spatial order, **I** for order of importance, or **L** for logical order.

_____ 1. The house, built in 1920, has an unusual layout.

_____ 2. The provinces of China share remarkable similarities in their governmental leadership and structure as well as remarkable differences in their populations and standards of living.

_____ 3. Ever since Fumiyo was young, she had trouble keeping track of her belongings.

_____ 4. When I get married, my spouse and I will follow certain rules of good communication.

_____ 5. The reading room of the Cooperville Library is often a cluttered, disorganized mess.

_____ 6. Between January and March there are five birthdays and two anniversaries in our family.

_____ 7. Three major systems in the body are the circulatory system, the respiratory system, and the digestive system.

_____ 8. Recent changes in the government of Vietnam have made it possible for people in that country to enjoy a better standard of living.

_____ 9. The history of ancient Korea deserves to be more well known.

_____ 10. Regular exercise results in four major benefits to your health and appearance.

HRW material copyrighted under notice appearing earlier in this work.

Chapter 1: Writing and Thinking

Writing a First Draft

There's no magic formula—no one right way—to write a first draft. However, you might consider these suggestions:

- Use your prewriting notes or outline as a guide.

- Write freely. Concentrate on expressing your ideas.

- Include any new ideas that come to you as you write.

- Don't worry about making errors in grammar, usage, and mechanics. You can fix them later.

Exercise Read the following prewriting notes about the Freedom Rides of the Civil Rights movement. Then write a paragraph about them. You may use as many of the details as you wish. You may also add details or comments.

Goal of the Freedom Rides—to challenge segregation on buses, in bus stations, in waiting rooms and lavatories, at lunch counters and drinking fountains

Sponsored by CORE—the Congress of Racial Equality

CORE, an integrated civil rights organization, created in 1942

Freedom Rides occurred on Trailways and Greyhound buses

Buses went from Washington, D.C. to Jackson, Mississippi, and New Orleans, Louisiana

Freedom rides first attempted in 1947—not successful

In 1961, CORE tried again, at time when SNCC, SCLC, and NAACP (civil rights organizations) were active

May 1961, black and white freedom riders firebombed and beaten in Alabama

Kennedy administration at first tried to stop rides, later provided police protection for the riders

_____

_____

_____

_____

_____

_____

_____

_____

_____

_____

HRW material copyrighted under notice appearing earlier in this work.

Chapter 1: Writing and Thinking

Peer Evaluation

Every writer needs an editor, a person who can read critically and with a different viewpoint. That's what a **peer evaluator** does. To evaluate the work of a classmate,

1. Tell the writer what's right as well as what's wrong.

2. Make suggestions for improvement. If you see a weakness, tell the writer how that weakness might be corrected.

3. Be sensitive to the writer's feelings. Offer constructive solutions, not negative criticism.

Exercise   Read the following paragraph. Then use the questions given below to write an evaluation of the paragraph.

Luis Muñoz Marín was the son of Puerto Rico's first premier. Luis Muñoz Marín lived in New York City. And went to school there. Luis Muñoz Marín lived in Washington DC too. Luis Muñoz Marín graduated from Gerogetown university. Luis Muñoz Marín became a senator. Luis Muñoz Marín became a governor.

1. What purpose does the paragraph serve? Does it fully accomplish its purpose?

2. What might the writer do to increase the sentence variety and to decrease the repetitiveness of the sentence structure?

3. What other problems might the writer address during revision and proofreading?

_____

_____

_____

_____

_____

_____

_____

_____

_____

_____

_____

_____

_____

HRW material copyrighted under notice appearing earlier in this work.

Chapter 1: Writing and Thinking

Revising by Adding and Cutting

Two revising techniques are adding and cutting.

You can **add** new information and details in new words, phrases, sentences, and paragraphs.

You can **cut** information, details, examples, or words. For example, you might cut repetition, wordiness, and details unrelated to the main idea.

Exercise   Study the revisions made to the following paragraph. Then answer the questions below.

One of the ~~neatest things~~ *most fascinating creatures* in ancient *Egyptian* mythology is the phoenix. This bird lived *magnificent gold and purple*

alone in the desert. ~~I wonder if they named the city of Phoenix, Arizona, after~~ *suddenly burst into flames.*   *from its own ashes*
~~this bird?~~ After living 500 to 600 years, it ~~died~~. But then it rose to live another

lifetime. That's why the phoenix is a symbol of immortality.

1. What details did the writer add to make the paragraph more vivid and concrete?

   _____

   _____

   _____

   _____

2. Why did the writer cross out the sentence, "I wonder if they named the city of

   Phoenix, Arizona, after this bird"?

   _____

   _____

HRW material copyrighted under notice appearing earlier in this work.

Chapter 1: Writing and Thinking

Revising by Replacing and Reordering

Two ways to revise are replacing and reordering.

You can **replace** weak words, clichés, awkward-sounding sentences, and unnecessary information or details.

You can **reorder** words, phrases, sentences, or paragraphs to add variety or to improve clarity.

Exercise   Study the revisions made to the following paragraph. Then answer the questions below.

Of these,
Swahili is the most widely spoken and understood ~~active language in Africa.~~

There are more than 800 native languages spoken on the continent of Africa. *Ki* is

a ~~word~~ *prefix* that makes the word ~~tell about~~ *refer to* a language instead of ~~about~~ *to* a people. The

actual name of the language is *Kiswahili.* ~~That means if you~~ *For example, a person who* speak*s* Swahili~~, you~~ *would*

refer to the language spoken by the Ganda people as "Kiganda" and the language

spoken by the Luo people as "Kiluo."

1. Why did the writer reorder the second sentence?

   _____

   _____

2. Why did the writer reorder the third sentence?

   _____

   _____

3. Why did the writer replace "word" with "prefix"?

   _____

   _____

4. Why did the writer replace "you" with "a person"?

   _____

   _____

HRW material copyrighted under notice appearing earlier in this work.

Proofreading

Proofreading is the process of checking your paper for mistakes in grammar, usage, and mechanics (including spelling, punctuation, capitalization). When you proofread, ask yourself the following questions:

1. Has the writer avoided sentence fragments and run-ons?

2. Does every sentence end with an appropriate end punctuation mark?

3. Does every sentence begin with a capital letter? Are all proper nouns and proper adjectives capitalized when necessary?

4. Does every verb agree in number with its subject?

5. Are verb forms and tenses used correctly?

6. Are subject and object forms of personal pronouns used correctly?

7. Does every pronoun agree in number and in gender with its antecedent? Are pronoun references clear?

8. Are frequently confused words (such as *lie* and *lay* or *imply* and *infer*) used correctly?

9. Are all words spelled correctly? Are the plural forms of nouns correct?

10. Is the paper neat and in correct manuscript form?

Exercise   Use the guidelines above to proofread the following paragraph. Correct the errors in grammar, usage, spelling, punctuation, and capitalization. Use a dictionary and the Handbook section of your textbook as necessary.

By 1656, Spanish missonaries, soldiers, and apalachee indians were living

together, peacefully and prosperously, in the settlement of San Luis de Talimali

in Northwest Florida. In 1704 the settlement which by then contained a large

apalachee counsel house, a church, a fort, and many homes came to an end the

inhabitants burn it to the ground as they flee British invaders. In 1983, when the

state of florida purchased San Luis, the village was, in a sense, reclamed from the

past. Today visitor's tour it's shady ground; and watch archaeologists as they

recover an important part of American History.

HRW material copyrighted under notice appearing earlier in this work.

Chapter 1: Writing and Thinking

Manuscript Form

When someone else is going to read your paper—a teacher, another student, or some adult outside the school—the appearance of the paper becomes quite important. Follow these guidelines when preparing your final copy.

Guidelines for Manuscript Form

1. Use only one side of a sheet of paper.

2. Use a typewriter or a word processor, or write in blue or black ink.

3. If you type, double-space the lines. If you write by hand, don't skip lines.

4. Leave margins of about one inch at the top, sides, and bottom of a page.

5. Indent the first line of each paragraph.

6. Number all pages, except the first page, in the upper right-hand corner.

7. All pages should be neat and clean. You may use correction fluid to make a few changes, but such changes should be barely noticeable.

8. Follow your teacher's instructions for placement of your name, the date, your class, and the title of your paper.

Exercise　How would you evaluate the manuscript form of the following final draft of a paragraph? Write your evaluation on a separate sheet of paper.

○	*Many Jewsih families came to American from Germany during the 1800s. A large number of these*
	immmigrants became peddlers who travelled from town to town selling goods. over time, and as
	they built up cash, some of thes peddlers used their knowledge of merchandise and sales to begin
	retail stores Some Jewish-American retail stores that grew from modest beginnings include Macy's
	and Gimbels in New York; Filene's in Boston; Lazarus, in Columbus, Ohio, and Meier and Frank in
	Portland, Oregon. Such successes are only a few examples of the innumurable contributions made
	by immigrants to America.
○	

HRW material copyrighted under notice appearing earlier in this work.

Chapter 1: Writing and Thinking

The Aim and Process of Writing

Aim — The "Why" of Writing

WHY PEOPLE WRITE	
To express themselves	To get to know themselves, to discover meaning in their own lives
To inform, to explain, or to explore	To give other people information they want or need; to provide an explanation; to explore an idea or problem
To persuade	To convince other people to do something or believe something
To create literary works	To be creative with language; to say something in a unique way

Process — The "How" of Writing

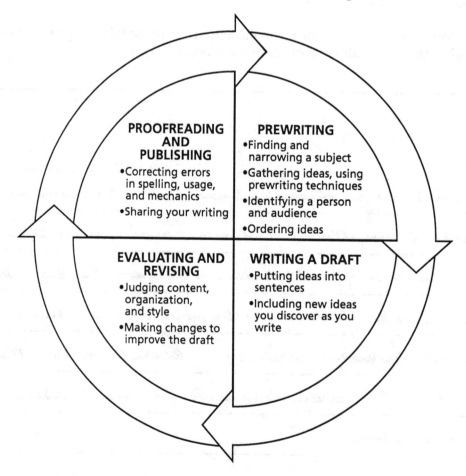

PROOFREADING AND PUBLISHING
•Correcting errors in spelling, usage, and mechanics
•Sharing your writing

PREWRITING
•Finding and narrowing a subject
•Gathering ideas, using prewriting techniques
•Identifying a person and audience
•Ordering ideas

EVALUATING AND REVISING
•Judging content, organization, and style
•Making changes to improve the draft

WRITING A DRAFT
•Putting ideas into sentences
•Including new ideas you discover as you write

HRW material copyrighted under notice appearing earlier in this work.

Answer Key

Practice and Reinforcement (1)
Freewriting and Brainstorming

Exercise A

(Answers will vary. A possible response is given.)

Subject chosen for brainstorming: shopping malls

Possible topics gathered from brainstorming: designs of malls, kinds of stores found in malls, going to the mall as a form of entertainment, what happened to downtown?, food courts, malls as gathering places for teenagers

Exercise B

(Answers will vary. A possible response is given.)

Malls. Endless shopfronts. Jewelry. Perfume. Candies. Fast food. Boom boxes. VCRs. "Can I help you?" Help! Teenagers roaming about. Cash registers printing out receipts. The shuttle sound of credit card machines. Temples of greed, mass market merchandise. Affluence for everyone. Or almost everyone. Malls as refuge for the homeless.

Practice and Reinforcement (2)
Clustering and Questioning

Exercise A

(Answers will vary. A possible response is given.)

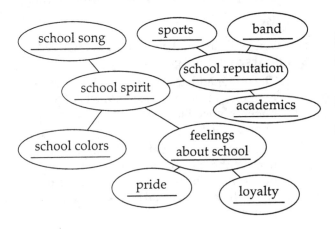

Exercise B

(Answers will vary. Possible responses are given.)

Subject: situation comedies

1. Who are the actors?
2. What is the typical format?
3. Where do the characters live, work, and go to school?
4. When do the most comic moments usually occur?
5. Why is the show so entertaining?
6. How does the show compare with others like it on TV?

Practice and Reinforcement (3)
Purpose, Audience, and Tone

Exercise

1. Purpose: to express feelings
   Audience: self
   Tone: upset, self-pitying
2. Purpose: to persuade
   Audience: someone interested in cars
   Tone: casual, cajoling
3. Purpose: to persuade
   Audience: people who make campfires
   Tone: sarcastic

Practice and Reinforcement (4)
Reading and Listening with a Focus

Exercise A

(Answers will vary. Possible responses are given.)

1. key words in the index: skyscrapers, elevators, Louis Sullivan
2. chapters worth reading: "The First Skyscraper"; "The Modern City Skyline"

HRW material copyrighted under notice appearing earlier in this work.

Answer Key

Exercise B

(Answers will vary. A possible response is given.)

The Wainwright Building

Chart: World's Tallest Buildings

Illustration: Plan of the New York business district

Photograph: Metropolitan Life Building

Problems and Solutions in the Pursuit of Height

Exercise C

(Answers will vary. A possible response is given.)

1. How long did the astronauts walk on the moon?
2. What was the most unexpected or delightful discovery on the moon's surface?
3. I want to know how Armstrong, Collins, and Aldrin were chosen for this particular mission.

Practice and Reinforcement (5)
Arranging Ideas

Exercise

1. S
2. L
3. C
4. I
5. S
6. C
7. L
8. C
9. I
10. I

Practice and Reinforcement (6)
Writing a First Draft

Exercise

(Answers will vary. A possible response is given.)

   The Freedom Rides of the 1960s were one of the courageous steps taken by blacks and whites committed to the ideal of racial equality. Organized by a group called CORE, the Congress of Racial Equality, Freedom Rides had been attempted as early as 1947, but it was not until 1961 that they began in the earnest way that eventually brought a measure of success. Freedom Rides occurred on Trailways and Greyhound buses traveling from Washington, D.C. to Jackson, Mississippi, and New Orleans, Louisiana. Their purpose was to challenge segregation on buses, in bus stations, in waiting rooms, in lavatories, at lunch counters, and at drinking fountains. Although the first ride met with violence, Freedom Riders eventually received police protection.

Practice and Reinforcement (7)
Peer Evaluation

Exercise

(Answers will vary. A possible response is given.)

1. The paragraph accomplishes its purpose— telling who Luis Marín was—and can in that sense be called successful.
2. It can be made even better by varying the openings of sentences.
3. There is one sentence fragment to be corrected, and there are a few minor errors in mechanics.

Practice and Reinforcement (8)
Revising by Adding and Cutting

Exercise

(Answers will vary in the way they are worded. Sample responses are given.)

1. The writer added details that tell which mythology is being discussed, what the phoenix looked like, and how, precisely, the phoenix died.
2. The writer cut the sentence because it is irrelevant to the main purpose of the paragraph, which is to provide information about the mythological bird known as the phoenix.

HRW material copyrighted under notice appearing earlier in this work.

Answer Key

Practice and Reinforcement (9)
Revising by Replacing and Reordering

Exercise

(Answers will vary in the way they are worded. Sample responses are given.)

1. The second sentence leads logically to the first sentence and not the other way around.
2. The third sentence helps explain the sentence that follows it and makes more sense if it is placed after it.
3. *Ki* is used in *Kiswahili* not as a whole word but as a word part.
4. The rest of the paragraph is written in the third person; the third person is appropriate for this type of information.

Practice and Reinforcement (10)
Proofreading

Exercise

By 1656, Spanish missionaries, soldiers, and apalachee indians were living together, peacefully and prosperously, in the settlement of San Luis de Talimali in Northwest Florida. In 1704 the settlement which by then contained a large apalachee counsel house, a church, a fort, and many homes came to an end the inhabitants burn it to the ground as they flee Brittish invaders. In 1983, when the state of florida purchased San Luis, the village was, in a sense, reclamed from the past. Today visitors tour its shady grounds and watch archaeologists as they recover an important part of American History.

Practice and Reinforcement (11)
Manuscript Form

Exercise

(Answers will vary. A sample response is given.)
This paragraph should be copied over, and the writer should do the following:

1. Leave margins of about one inch all sides of the page.
2. Indent the paragraph.
3. Neatly correct the errors in spelling and mechanics.
4. Make the existing correction neater.

HRW material copyrighted under notice appearing earlier in this work.

Using Short Paragraphs Effectively

Some paragraphs are made up of many sentences. Others are quite short. In some cases paragraphs are no more than one or two sentences long. A one- or two-sentence paragraph can be used to call attention to a single point, to make a transition, to catch the reader's eye, to break up writing into small units to make it easier to read, to show that a person is speaking, or to conclude the piece of writing.

Exercise   Read the following passage. Then, on the lines provided, write one possible use of each numbered paragraph. Some paragraphs may have more than one use.

(1) Firerolet Millenium is the new luxury class car to buy this season.

(2) The height of styling and luxury inside and out, the Firerolet features an automatic, self-adjusting steering wheel that rises when you leave the car and lowers when you enter it.

(3) What else does this car offer?

(4) Features include an interior of fine, upholstered leather.

(5) And this car will give you the quietest, most comfortable ride you've ever taken.

(6) Says Millenium owner Joanna Ruiz, "It's everything I've ever wanted in a car."

(7) The Millenium. Drive one today.

1. _____
   _____

2. _____
   _____

3. _____
   _____

4. _____
   _____

5. _____
   _____

6. _____
   _____

7. _____
   _____

HRW material copyrighted under notice appearing earlier in this work.

Chapter 2: Understanding Paragraph Structure

Main Ideas and Topic Sentences

Paragraphs in thoughtful articles and in other works of nonfiction, such as the essays that you write in school, usually develop one main idea. These main idea paragraphs often—but do not always—contain a topic sentence. The **topic sentence** is a specific, limiting statement about the subject of the paragraph. Although a topic sentence can appear at any place in the paragraph, it often appears as the first or second sentence.

Exercise   On the lines provided, write the main idea and topic sentence of each paragraph. If the paragraph does not have a topic sentence, write *No Topic Sentence.*

1. For the Sioux, as for many other resettled Native Americans, reservation life was miserable. Christian missionaries there questioned and often attacked their beliefs. Ceremonies such as the Sun Dance were banned. The Sioux were no longer able to roam and to hunt. Their very food and clothing changed.

Main idea: _____

Topic sentence: _____

2. One day a Sioux named Yellow Hair approached one of the agents from the Indian Bureau who ran the Pine Ridge reservation. Yellow Hair picked up some earth, rolled it into a ball, and gave it to the agent. "We have given up nearly all our land," said Yellow Hair, "and you had better take the balance now here…, I hand it to you."

Main idea: _____

Topic sentence: _____

3. Defeated Native Americans were given areas of land called reservations. Yet they did not even have control over their reservations. The reservations were run instead by agents from the Indian Bureau. For example, the Native Americans did not divide up the land themselves. Instead, the Dawes Act divided the land into plots for each family so that the Native Americans would farm in the same way that the white settlers farmed.

Main idea: _____

Topic sentence: _____

4. Where was the honor and dignity of life on a reservation? Who could feel satisfied with a life where one had to stand in long lines to receive poor quality food and clothing? Who could feel satisfied when there were no longer buffalo and where life could not change with the seasons? Out of such conditions grew despair and misery.

Main idea: _____

Topic sentence: _____

HRW material copyrighted under notice appearing earlier in this work.

Chapter 2: Understanding Paragraph Structure

Using Details

The main idea or topic sentence of a paragraph usually needs to be supported with additional information. Two ways to support a main idea are with sensory details and with facts and statistics.

Sensory details are images of sight, sound, smell, taste, and texture. They can be used to bring a subject to life for readers.

A **fact** is a statement that can be proved true.

> John F. Kennedy became the first Irish-Catholic president of the United States.

A **statistic** is a fact that involves numbers.

> More than 40 million Americans claim Irish descent.

Exercise A   Choose one of the following topics or one of your own. On the lines provided, write the topic and five sensory details related to the topic. If possible, write one detail for each of the five senses.

> **Possible Topics:** my dream vacation; my grandparents' cellar, attic, condo, or farm; downtown; the ideal dance or prom; a favorite holiday

Topic: _____

1. _____

2. _____

3. _____

4. _____

5. _____

Exercise B   Choose one of the following topics or one of your own. On the lines provided, write your topic and three facts or statistics that you could use to support your topic.

> **Possible topics:** the best sporting goods store; the best CD store; an outstanding athlete, film star, inventor; why your state, city, or county is a great place to live

Topic: _____

1. _____

   _____

2. _____

   _____

3. _____

   _____

HRW material copyrighted under notice appearing earlier in this work.

Chapter 2: Understanding Paragraph Structure

Using Examples and Anecdotes

To make the main idea of a paragraph clear, you may have to develop that idea in detail. Two ways to elaborate on a main idea are with examples and anecdotes.

Examples are specific instances or illustrations of a general idea.

> **General idea:** Thai food offers many interesting flavors.

> **Example:** Lemon grass, an unusual herb used in Thai food, has a tangy, aromatic flavor.

An **anecdote** is a little story that is usually biographical or autobiographical.

> **Main idea:** Mark Twain's sense of humor was always at work.

> **Anecdote:** When Twain lived in Hartford, Connecticut, his mansion was among the largest and most ornate in the country and included, even during the cold northeastern winters, an indoor greenhouse. Twain was not, however, always able to keep up with the expenses of his lavish lifestyle. So it was that he enjoyed his billiards room, which had a small veranda. When bill collectors would call, Twain would step out onto the veranda and instruct a servant to tell the bill collector, "Mr. Twain has just stepped out."

Exercise A   Choose one of the following topics or one of your own. Write the general idea and two sentences that present examples related to the topic.

> **Possible topics:** bicycling is the best individual sport; the worst show on TV this season; aerobic dancing is the best for exercise; chess is the most challenging board game; a good way to learn a second language is by watching movies and television in that language

General idea: _____

  1. _____

  2. _____

Exercise B   Choose one of the following main ideas or one of your own. Underline your main idea. Then write an anecdote to support it.

> **Possible main ideas:** I was a creative child; taking a chance paid off for me, my sister, my grandfather; good people often do finish first

Anecdote: _____

_____

_____

_____

_____

_____

HRW material copyrighted under notice appearing earlier in this work.

Chapter 2: Understanding Paragraph Structure

The Clincher Sentence

A **clincher sentence** is a final sentence that emphasizes or summarizes the main idea of a paragraph.

Exercise   For each of the following paragraphs, write an appropriate clincher sentence.

1. Twice each year the clothing industry tries to convince people that their clothes are out of fashion and that they need to buy the latest designs. In March an army of fashion writers and photographers attends showings of fall and winter clothes in Milan. They travel on to London and Paris later that month and to New York in April. Spring and summer clothes are shown beginning in October, also in Milan, Paris, London, and New York. Designers, manufacturers, and retail store owners wait nervously to see what fashion writers choose to adore or to scorn.

Clincher sentence: _____

_____

2. From the minute we wake up to the minute we fall asleep, we are bombarded by information about our world. Some of this information is presented in news broadcasts on radio and television. Some comes from books, newspapers, and magazines. And as if radio, television, books, newspapers, and magazines were not enough, we now have computers that can bring whole libraries of information into our own homes.

Clincher sentence: _____

_____

3. In recent years doctors have been urging people to eat low-fat, low-cholesterol diets. One result has been the creation of new cereals for adults, including "natural" and high-fiber cereals. These cereals often contain honey instead of sugar and whole grains instead of refined grains. Bran flakes and other forms of bran are also increasingly popular as breakfast foods.

Clincher sentence: _____

_____

HRW material copyrighted under notice appearing earlier in this work.

Chapter 2: Understanding Paragraph Structure

Achieving Unity

When a paragraph has **unity,** all the supporting sentences work together to develop the main idea. A paragraph should have unity whether the main idea is stated in a topic sentence or is implied (suggested).

In paragraphs that relate a series of actions or events, the main idea is often implied rather than stated. You can achieve unity in such paragraphs by using a logical sequence of actions or events.

Exercise Each of the following paragraphs contains one sentence that destroys its unity. Find that unrelated sentence in each paragraph and draw a line through it.

1. Extracurricular activities help develop well-rounded personalities. In many clubs or teams, members learn cooperation and leadership. Dues are low, and there are few if any entrance requirements. Working on school newspapers, yearbooks, and dramatic productions teaches responsibility toward others and the ability to meet a schedule or deadline. Such activities help students develop talents that might otherwise remain undiscovered or undeveloped.

2. Polio, once a killer and crippler of adults and children, fell to the Salk and Sabine vaccines. Measles, once an inevitable experience during childhood, can now be totally avoided with proper immunization. Many diseases did not exist in North America until the Europeans brought them here. Smallpox, once a dreaded killer worldwide, is now virtually unheard of. Thanks to vaccines, these and many other diseases are now for the most part historical curiosities.

3. Scientists who work in the field of artificial intelligence, or AI, are concentrating their energies on replicating some seemingly simple but actually quite complicated human abilities. Some AI researchers are trying to teach machines how to recognize patterns. Others are attempting to write programs that imitate natural human language. Still others are working on manual skills and locomotion. In recent years computers have gotten much, much smaller than they were in the 1950s and '60s.

HRW material copyrighted under notice appearing earlier in this work.

Chapter 2: Understanding Paragraph Structure

Achieving Coherence

A paragraph has **coherence** when its ideas are clearly connected. You can connect ideas by using direct references or transitional words and phrases.

Direct references are words that refer to or that are are synonymous with nouns or pronouns that have appeared earlier.

Transitional words and phrases tell how one idea is related to another. They indicate time, place, importance, comparison, contrast, classification, definition, description, evaluation, and summation.

In the following paragraph the direct references are shown in **boldface.** The transitional words and phrases are *italicized.*

> In 1936 a Mexican American named **Joseph Montoya** was elected to the house of representatives of his home state, **New Mexico.** *At that time* **Montoya,** a **Democrat,** was only twenty-one years of age. **That election** made him the youngest man *ever* to be seated on the **state legislature.** *Two years later* **he** was reelected. *During the same year* he was named the majority floor leader. *Later,* **Montoya** was elected to the state senate; *subsequently,* **he** became the **lieutenant governor** of **his state.**

Exercise   On the lines provided, list the direct references and transitional words and phrases in the paragraph below.

> Joseph Montoya's most important political victory occurred in 1964. During that year Montoya was elected to the United States Senate. While he was a U.S. senator, he involved himself in the Civil Rights Movement. It was not until 1973, however, that Montoya was thrust into the national limelight. The senator from New Mexico quickly became a prominent national figure when the committee on which he served investigated the Watergate scandal.

Direct References   **Transitional Words and Phrases**

_____ _____   _____ _____

_____ _____   _____ _____

_____ _____   _____ _____

_____ _____   _____ _____

_____ _____   _____ _____

_____ _____   _____ _____

_____ _____   _____ _____

HRW material copyrighted under notice appearing earlier in this work.

Chapter 1: Understanding Paragraph Structure

Using Description and Narration

Two ways to develop a paragraph are by using description and narration. **Description** is a strategy of development that looks at the individual features of one or more subjects. Description uses many sensory details. **Narration** is a strategy of development that looks at changes in a subject over a period of time. You may use narration to tell a story, to explain a process, or to explain causes and effects.

Exercise A   Select one of the following topic sentences or one of your own. Use the topic sentence as a starting point for brainstorming sensory details that you could use to develop a descriptive paragraph.

1. I've always loved amusement parks.

2. The best pet my family ever had was a confused little mutt called Alfredito.

Topic sentence: _____

Details: _____   _____

        _____   _____

        _____   _____

        _____   _____

Exercise B   Select one of the following topics for a story or one of your own. Brainstorm a list of events that you could include in a narrative paragraph on the topic.

        Topics: my trip to (any place), my battle with (anything you confronted or overcame), the worst day I ever had

Topic: _____

Events: _____

        _____

        _____

Exercise C   Select one of the following topics for a cause-and-effect paragraph or one of your own. Brainstorm a list of causes and effects that you could include in a narrative paragraph on the topic.

        Topics: why I had such a (good, bad) grading period

        how I managed to (an accomplishment or victory)

Topic: _____

Causes: Effects:

_____   _____

_____   _____

_____   _____

HRW material copyrighted under notice appearing earlier in this work.

Chapter 2: Understanding Paragraph Structure

Classification and Evaluation

Two ways to develop paragraphs are by using classification and evaluation. **Classification** is a strategy of development that looks at a subject in relation to other subjects. There are three ways to classify: divide a subject into its parts, define it, or compare and contrast it with something else.

Evaluation is a strategy of development that analyzes or judges the value of a subject. Evaluation uses reasons to support the judgment.

Exercise A   Select one of the following topics or one of your own. Write three or more parts into which the topic could be divided.

> **Topics:** a child's education   the senior year
>
> the baseball season   adulthood

Topic: _____

Parts: _____   _____

_____   _____

Exercise B   Select one of the following topics or one of your own. Write the name of the larger group or class to which your topic belongs. Then list three details that distinguish the topic from other members of that group or class.

> **Topics:** jets   haunted houses at amusement parks
>
> pizza   jazz

Topic: _____

Larger group or class: _____

Details: _____

_____

_____

Exercise C   Select one of the following topic sentences or one of your own. Use the topic sentence as a starting point for brainstorming three reasons that you could present in an evaluative paragraph.

1. A jacket is the most important fashion item in a wardrobe.

2. Getting proper exercise is the best route to good health.

Topic sentence: _____

1. _____

2. _____

3. _____

HRW material copyrighted under notice appearing earlier in this work.

Transitional Words and Phrases

Whether your piece of writing is made up of a single paragraph or many paragraphs, you will always be connecting ideas. The following chart is a handy guide to words that make the right connections.

TRANSITIONAL WORDS AND PHRASES		
Comparing Ideas/Classification and Definition		
also	another	similarly
and	moreover	too
Contrasting Ideas/Classification and Definition		
although	in spite of	on the other
but	nevertheless	hand
however		still
		yet
Showing Cause and Effect/Narration		
as a result	consequently	so that
because	since	therefore
Showing Time/Narration		
after	eventually	next
at last	finally	then
at once	first	thereafter
before	meanwhile	
Showing Place/Description		
above	down	next
across	here	over
around	in	there
before	inside	to
beyond	into	under
Showing Importance/Evaluation		
first	mainly	then
last	more important	to begin with

HRW material copyrighted under notice appearing earlier in this work.

Answer Key

Practice and Reinforcement (1)
Using Short Paragraphs Effectively

Exercise

(Students need provide only one of all the possible answers given for each item.)

1. to call attention to a single point, to catch the reader's eye
2. to call attention to a single point, to catch the reader's eye, to break up writing into small units to make it easier to read
3. to make a transition
4. to call attention to a single point, to catch the reader's eye, to break up writing into small units to make it easier to read
5. to call attention to a single point, to catch the reader's eye, to break up writing into small units to make it easier to read
6. to show that a person is speaking, to call attention to a single point, to catch the reader's eye, to break up writing into small units to make it easier to read
7. to conclude the piece of writing

Practice and Reinforcement (2)
Main Ideas and Topic Sentences

Exercise

1. Main idea: life on a Sioux reservation
   Topic Sentence: For the Sioux, as for many other resettled Native Americans, reservation life was miserable
2. Main idea: the whites taking the land from the Sioux
   Topic Sentence: No topic sentence
3. Main idea: the Native Americans didn't control their own reservation
   Topic Sentence: Yet they did not even have control over their reservations
4. Main idea: the honor and dignity of reservation life
   Topic Sentence: Where was the honor and dignity of life on a reservation?

Practice and Reinforcement (3)
Using Details

Exercise A

(Answers will vary. Possible responses are given.)
Topic: my grandparents' farm
Sight: huge cornfields
Sound: the sound of the tractor
Touch: patting a horse
Taste: apples fresh from their trees
Smell: fresh hay

Exercise B

(Answers will vary. Possible responses are given.)
Topic: the best sporting goods store

1. offers more than 40 brands of running shoes and athletic shoes
2. offers a 14-day, no questions asked, money-back guarantee
3. regularly offers 25 percent sales on all merchandise, not just on what doesn't sell

Practice and Reinforcement (4)
Using Examples and Anecdotes

Exercise A

(Answers will vary. Possible responses are given.)
General idea: A good way to learn a second language is by watching movies and television in that language.

1. Television movies, sitcoms, and dramas present the language as it is actually spoken.
2. Television and videos are readily available; you don't have to find someone to converse with.

HRW material copyrighted under notice appearing earlier in this work.

Answer Key

Exercise B

(Answers will vary. A possible response is given.)

Main idea: Taking a chance paid off for my grandfather.

Anecdote: My grandfather left Italy in the 1930s, just before the war. It was a gamble for him. He had to leave behind everything he knew: his family, his friends, his city, even his language. He came to America, got a job on the railroad, and worked hard for many years. Eventually, he was able to buy a house and send his kids to college.

Practice and Reinforcement (5)
The Clincher Sentence

Exercise

(Students' clincher sentences will vary. Possible responses are given.)

1. Persuading the public that their clothes are out of date is a complicated process involving thousands of people.

2. There's no question about it—we are a nation of information addicts.

3. The days of eggs and bacon, sausage and home fries may be gone for good.

Practice and Reinforcement (6)
Achieving Unity

Exercise A

1. ~~Dues are low, and there are few if any entrance requirements.~~

2. ~~Many diseases did not exist in North America until the Europeans brought them here.~~

3. ~~In recent years computers have gotten much, much smaller than they were in the 1950s and '60s.~~

Practice and Reinforcement (7)
Achieving Coherence

Exercise

Direct References	Transitional Words and phrases
that year	in
Montoya	During
he	to
U.S. senator	While
he	in
himself	until
Montoya	however
senator	into
prominent national figure	from
he	quickly
	when
	on which

Practice and Reinforcement (8)
Using Description and Narration

Exercise A

(Answers will vary. Possible responses are given.)

Topic sentence: The best pet my family ever had was a confused little mutt called Alfredito.

Details: soft and cuddly

high-pitched yapping

bad habit of knocking over trash cans and smelling bad later

long floppy ears, long hair, thin tail

very fast runner

cold, wet nose

HRW material copyrighted under notice appearing earlier in this work.

Answer Key

Exercise B

(Answers will vary. Possible responses are given.)

Topic: the worst day I ever had

1. Rehearsed for weeks for school play.
2. Opening night, got stage fright.
3. Forgot my lines.
4. Understudy had to take over.

Exercise C

(Answers will vary. Possible responses are given.)

Topic: How I improved from D in math to B

Causes	Effects
received a D	my parents upset
talked with the teacher	created a study plan
studied extra every night	improved my test scores

Practice and Reinforcement (9)
Classification and Evaluation

Exercise A

(Answers will vary. Possible responses are given.)

Topic: the senior year

Parts: first three months of excitement, hard work, college applications

next two months people start making decisions about next year

next two or three months hard to keep up interest in school, thinking about the future

last two months of class trips, dances, preparations for graduation

Exercise B

(Answers will vary. Possible responses are given.)

Topic: pizza

Larger group or class: dinner foods

Details: can eat with hands

inexpensive

easy to get

delicious combination of bread, cheese, and sauce

many variations possible

Exercise C

(Answers will vary. Possible responses are given.)

Topic Sentence: A jacket is the most important fashion item in a wardrobe.

1. A jacket is worn constantly—more than most other items of clothing.
2. A jacket is seen in public, so it gets more exposure than other items of clothing.
3. A jacket is large—bigger than, say, a blouse or pants—and therefore meets the eye faster and is more obvious.

HRW material copyrighted under notice appearing earlier in this work.

Chapter 3: Understanding Composition Structure

The Thesis Statement

When you write a composition, you generally have a particular point to make about your limited topic. This point is your **thesis,** and the sentence that you write to express this main idea is your **thesis statement.**

Exercise A   On the lines provided, identify the limited topic for each of the following thesis statements.

1. Vicksburg, not Gettysburg, was the most important battle of the Civil War.

Limited topic: _____

2. Selecting proper jogging shoes has become a complicated, time-consuming process.

Limited topic: _____

3. The excavation of the tomb of King Tutankhamen in 1923 provided a fascinating glimpse into life in ancient Egypt.

Limited topic: _____

4. The Aztecs built magnificent cities.

Limited topic: _____

Exercise B   On the lines provided, write a thesis statement for each of the following sets of details.

1. **Limited topic:** nineteenth-century immigrant workers

    Details:

        dirty, dangerous conditions in factories

        danger in mines

        frequent accidents in mills

Thesis statement: _____

_____

_____

2. **Limited topic:** board games

    Details:

        backgammon a war game involving strategy and opposing forces

        chess a war game involving strategy and opposing forces

Thesis statement: _____

_____

_____

HRW material copyrighted under notice appearing earlier in this work.

Chapter 3: Understanding Composition Structure

Early Plans

An **early plan**, sometimes called a **rough** or **informal outline**, records the gist of the information that will appear in a composition.

To prepare an early plan, first group your ideas. Then order them. To group ideas,

Sort related ideas and details into separate groups.

Make a separate list of details that don't fit into any group.

Give each group a separate label.

If you are writing about events over time, you'll probably use **chronological** (time) **order.** If you are describing something, you'll probably use **spatial** (space) **order.** If you're comparing and contrasting, you'll use **logical order.**

Exercise A   On the lines provided, organize the following details into two groups. Above each group of details, write a heading that identifies what the details have in common.

sits, heels   big brown eyes   long, floppy ears

a long, thin body   fetches the newspaper   rolls over

short, bobbed tail

_____   _____

_____   _____

_____   _____

_____   _____

Exercise B   Identify the details from the list above that relate to the dog's appearance. On the first line below, explain one way of putting these details in spatial order (for example, from left to right). Then list the details in that order.

Order: _____   _____

1. _____

2. _____

3. _____

4. _____

HRW material copyrighted under notice appearing earlier in this work.

Formal Outlines

One way to arrange your ideas is to create a formal outline. A **formal outline** has numerals and letters that identify headings and subheadings. It may be a topic outline, which uses single words or phrases, or a **sentence outline,** which uses complete sentences.

Exercise A   Complete the topic outline below by filling in information from the following list.

Pay television   New office technologies

New entertainment technologies   Computer games

Fax modems

I. _____

  A. _____

  B. Cable television

  C. Virtual reality arcade games

  D. Laser discs

  E. _____

  F. Digital movies

II. _____

  A. Facsimile machines

  B. Modems

  C. _____

  D. Personal computers

  E. Laptop computers

  F. Computer networks

Exercise B   Write a thesis statement based on the outline given above. _____

_____

_____

_____

_____

HRW material copyrighted under notice appearing earlier in this work.

The Introduction

An effective **introduction** catches the reader's attention, sets the tone of the composition, and presents the thesis. The **tone** is the emotional stance of the writer (humorous, critical, serious, etc.)

Techniques for writing introductions include addressing the reader directly, relating an anecdote or example, presenting an unusual or enlightening fact, asking a question, posing a challenge, taking a stand on some issue, making an outrageous or comical statement, and simply stating the thesis. Many introductions use a combination of these techniques.

Exercise For each of the following introductions, identify the thesis statement, the tone, and the technique used for writing the introduction.

1. According to E. O. Wilson of Harvard University, the ants and other insects on our planet outweigh us by about twelve to one. So, for every one-hundred-and-fifty-pound person on earth, there are about 1,800 pounds of beetles, flies, ants, wasps, gnats, cockroaches, and other creatures that you don't want to invite in for dinner.

Think about that 1,800-pound figure for a minute. A single insect weighs less than the shadow of a grimace. So how many insects does it take to equal 1,800 pounds? Kids have a word for it—Gazillions. That's how many insects showed up in my tent the last time I went camping. It's a sport that I recommend highly—to people I don't like very much.

Thesis statement: _____

Tone: _____

Technique: _____

2. You are about to take an amazing journey through the human body. This journey begins with your heart, a powerful pump that sends five liters or more of blood through your body every minute. The journey includes stopovers in your lungs, your arteries and veins, your capillaries, and every cell in your body. What is the pathway that you will travel on? It is your circulatory system. The circulatory system is one of the most important transportation networks in your body.

Thesis statement: _____

Tone: _____

Technique: _____

HRW material copyrighted under notice appearing earlier in this work.

Chapter 3: Understanding Composition Structure

The Body

The **body** of a composition is the part where you develop your main idea. The body should have both unity and coherence.

When a composition has **unity**, every paragraph and every detail supports a single main idea. When a composition has **coherence**, direct references and transitional words and phrases have been used to link ideas. Direct references are nouns or pronouns that repeat key words or that refer back to them. Transitional words and phrases, such as *for example, therefore, meanwhile,* and *second,* logically connect sentences and paragraphs to one another.

Exercise   The following paragraphs form part of the body of a composition. Add transitional words and phrases and direct references on the lines provided. Circle any sentence that is out of order and draw an arrow to show where it belongs. Cross out any sentence that does not directly relate to the topic of its paragraph.

In 1889, _____ Rudyard Kipling was 24 years old, he decided to visit the

United States. _____ he would win the Nobel Prize for Literature in 1907, in

1889 _____ was a virtually unknown newspaper reporter. One of his aims in

visiting the United States was to interview Mark Twain, _____ had achieved

international fame.

Kipling had a hard time finding Mark Twain. In Buffalo someone told

_____ to try Hartford; someone else said to try Europe. A third person said to

go to Elmira. _____ , Kipling boarded a train for Elmira, reached _____ at

midnight, and was told that _____ was probably not in town.

That was wrong, _____ . After a little sleuthing, Kipling learned where

Twain lived. Kipling is probably best known for his famous *Jungle Book.* Arriving

finally at Twain's house, Quarry Farm, Kipling was told, "Mr. Clemens has just gone

downtown." Of Kipling, Twain later said: "Between us, we cover all knowledge. He

knows all that can be known, and _____ know the rest."

Back to town the journalist went. When Kipling _____ found the great man,

Kipling was excited and exhausted. Twain, _____ , very calmly invited him in

to chat.

And that is just what _____ did. Twain told stories about his upbringing,

commented on his writing, and discussed publishers and copyrights. _____ the

end of the interview, Kipling had plenty of material for a superb article.

HRW material copyrighted under notice appearing earlier in this work.

Chapter 3: Understanding Composition Structure

The Conclusion

A composition needs a satisfying ending, or **conclusion.** Readers need to feel that the ideas in the composition are tied together and complete.

To create an effective conclusion, choose from among these techniques:

1. Refer back to the introduction.

2. Offer a solution.

3. Restate your thesis.

4. Summarize your major points.

5. Provide an example of your main idea.

6. Personally comment on your topic.

7. Pose a dramatic question or challenge.

Exercise   On the lines provided, identify the techniques used by the writers of the following conclusions.

1. Technological advances in preparation, storage, and distribution processes help ensure that the food we grow will be used efficiently. Such advances even out the natural cycles of bounty and shortage and make modern society possible.

Technique: _____

2. We began by asking the question, "Why were the Easter Island statues built?" We are forced to admit that, while we have some tantalizing clues, we still have no definitive answer.

Technique: _____

3. Although the damage to the ozone is severe and will not be readily reversed, this is not time for the "I-can't-make-a-difference" attitude. Indeed, you can and must attempt to make a difference. Begin by writing to your congressional representatives today.

Technique: _____

4. In the 1970s and '80s, dramatic progress was made in increasing children's awareness of the dangers of cigarette smoking. Yet teenage smoking among some socioeconomic groups is actually on the rise. The solution to this problem may lie in renewed emphasis on and commitment to early childhood education about smoking.

Technique: _____

HRW material copyrighted under notice appearing earlier in this work.

Chapter 3: Understanding Composition Structure

Revising and Proofreading

Writers and editors use the following symbols as handy shortcuts when they revise and proofread. Using these symbols will make your writing and editing tasks easier, too.

SYMBOLS FOR REVISING AND PROOFREADING		
SYMBOL	**EXAMPLE**	**MEANING OF SYMBOL**
cap ≡	Spence college	Capitalize a lowercase letter.
lc /	our Best quarterback	Lowercase a capital letter.
∧	on Fourth of July	Insert a missing word, letter, or punctuation mark.
/	endurence	Change a letter.
∧	the capital of Iowa	Change a word.
?	hoped for to go	Leave out a word, letter, or punctuation mark.
?	on that occassion	Leave out and close up.
⌒	today's home work	Close up space.
∩	nieghbor	Change the order of letters.
tr ∩	the counsel general of the corporation	Transpose the circled words. (Write *tr* in nearby margin.)
¶	¶"Wait!" I shouted.	Begin a new paragraph.
⊙	She was right⊙	Add a period.
∧	Yes that's true.	Add a comma.
#	centerfield	Add a space.
⊙	the following items⊙	Add a colon.
∧	Evansville, Indiana Columbus, Ohio	Add a semicolon.
=	self=control	Add a hyphen.
∨	Mrs. Ruizs office	Add an apostrophe.
stet	a very tall building	Keep the crossed-out material. (Write *stet* in nearby margin.)

HRW material copyrighted under notice appearing earlier in this work.

Answer Key

Practice and Reinforcement (1)
The Thesis Statement

Exercise A

(Answers may vary in the way they are worded. Possible responses are given.)

1. Limited topic: Battle of Vicksburg
2. Limited topic: selecting jogging shoes
3. Limited topic: the excavation of the tomb of King Tut
4. Limited topic: Aztec cities

Exercise B

(Answers will vary. A possible response is given.)

1. Nineteenth-century immigrants labored under dangerous conditions in factories, mines, and mills.
2. Backgammon and chess are war games involving strategy and opposing forces.

Practice and Reinforcement (2)
Early Plans

Exercise A

(Answers will vary. Possible responses are given.)

Heading: Appearance
long, floppy ears
short, bobbed tail
long, thin body
big brown eyes

Heading: Tricks
sits, heels
rolls over
fetches the newspaper

Exercise B

(Answers will vary. A possible response is given.)

Order: from head to tail

1. long, floppy ears
2. big, brown eyes
3. long, thin body
4. short, bobbed tail

Practice and Reinforcement (3)
Formal Outlines

Exercise A

I. New entertainment technologies
   A. Pay television
   B. Cable television
   C. Virtual reality arcade games
   D. Laser discs
   E. Computer games
   F. Digital movies

II. New office technologies
   A. Facsimile machines
   B. Modems
   C. Fax modems
   D. Personal computers
   E. Laptop computers
   F. Computer networks

Exercise B

(Answers will vary. A possible response is given.)

Many exciting new technologies have changed everday life in late twentieth-century America.

Practice and Reinforcement (4)
The Introduction

1. Thesis statement: It's a sport that I recommend highly—to people I don't like very much.

   Tone: informal, humorous

   Technique: begins with unusual fact, makes some comical statements

2. Thesis statement: The circulatory system is one of the most important transportation networks in your body.

   Tone: amazement and wonder, informal

   Technique: addressing the reader directly

HRW material copyrighted under notice appearing earlier in this work.

Answer Key

Practice and Reinforcement (5)
The Body

Exercise

(Answers will vary. Possible responses are given.)

In 1889, when Rudyard Kipling was 24 years old, he decided to visit the United States. Although he would win the Nobel Prize for Literature in 1907, in 1889 he was a virtually unknown newspaper reporter. One of his aims in visiting the United States was to interview Mark Twain, who had achieved international fame.

Kipling had a hard time finding Mark Twain. In Buffalo someone told him to try Hartford; someone else said to try Europe. A third person said to go to Elmira. Therefore, Kipling boarded a train for Elmira, reached the city at midnight, and was told that Twain was probably not in town.

That was wrong, however. After a little sleuthing, Kipling learned where Twain lived. ~~Kipling is probably best known for his famous Jungle Book.~~ Arriving finally at Twain's house, Quarry Farm, Kipling was told, "Mr. Clemens has just gone downtown." Of Kipling, Twain later said: "Between us, we cover all knowledge. He knows all that can be known, and I know the rest.

Back to town the journalist went. When Kipling finally found the great man, Kipling was excited and exhausted. Twain, on the other hand, very calmly invited him to chat.

And that is what they did. Twain told stories about his upbringing, commented on his writing, and discussed publishers and copyrights. By the end of the interview, Kipling had plenty of material for a superb article.

Practice and Reinforcement (6)
The Conclusion

Exercise

1. summarizing major points
2. referring back to the introduction, posing a dramatic question
3. posing a challenge
4. offering a solution

HRW material copyrighted under notice appearing earlier in this work.